Footprints in the Sand

Design by Anne Van Wagner Childs

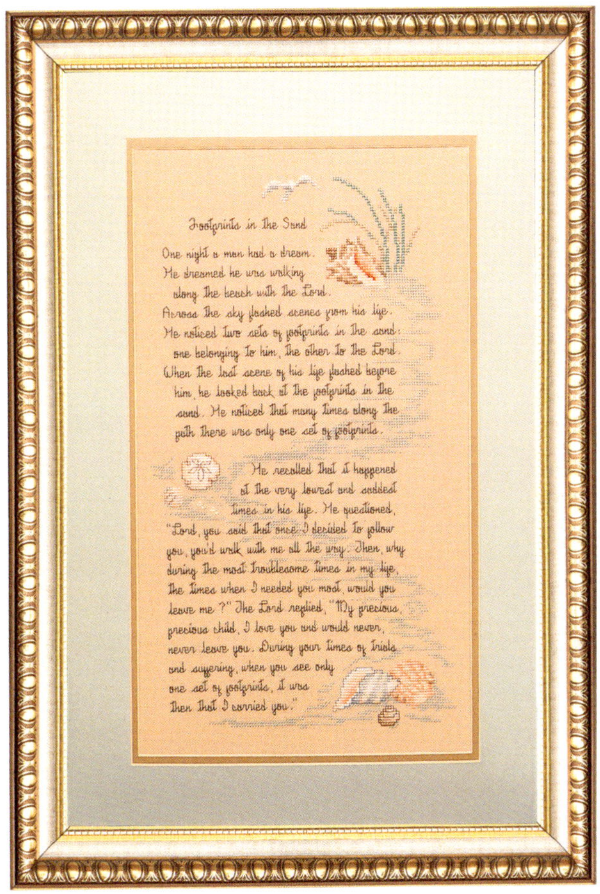

Table of Contents

Leisure Arts Inc. • Maumelle Arkansas

FOOTPRINTS IN THE SAND (114w x 197h)	
Aida 11 or Hardanger 22 over 2	10⅜" x 18"
Aida 14	8¼" x 14⅛"
Aida 18	6⅜" x 11"
Hardanger 22	5¼" x 9"

Grey shaded area indicates last row stitched on top section.

FOOTPRINTS IN THE SAND (114w x 197h)

ANCHOR	X	DMC	½X	B'ST	COLOR
02	⬚	blanc			white
0387	O	ecru			ecru
0778	–	948			lt peach
0868	◇	754			peach
9575	☆	758			dk peach
5975	V	356			lt rust
5968	✱	355			rust
0858	◎	524			lt green
0875	+	503			lt blue green
0849		927	▢		grey blue
0933	S	543			beige
0376	▫	842			vy lt beige brown
0378	X	841			lt beige brown
0379	△	840		/	beige brown
0936		839		/	dk beige brown
0380		838		/	vy dk beige brown
0397	C	762			lt grey
0398	✦	415			grey
0399	■	318			dk grey
0400		414		/	vy dk grey

GENERAL INSTRUCTIONS

WORKING WITH CHART

How To Read Chart: The design is shown in chart form. Each colored square on the chart **with a symbol** represents one Cross Stitch (except when a Backstitch line crosses the colored square and there is no space for symbol). Each colored square on the chart **without a symbol** represents one Half Cross Stitch. This method of charting with color enables you to see approximately how the design will look. The straight lines on the chart indicate Backstitch. These lines are shown either in color or black; the color to use is indicated on the color key.

How To Determine Finished Size: The finished size of the design depends on the **thread count per inch** of the fabric being used. To determine the finished size of the design on different fabrics, divide the number of squares (stitches) in the width of the charted design by the thread count of the fabric. For example: This design, which has a width of 114 squares, will be approximately 8¼" wide when worked on Aida 14 fabric. Repeat for the number of squares (stitches) in the height of the charted design. (***Note:*** To work over two fabric threads, divide the number of squares by one-half the thread count.) Then add the amount of background you want plus a generous amount for finishing.

Where To Start: The horizontal and vertical centers of the charted design are shown by arrows. You may start at any point on the charted design, but be sure the design will be centered on the fabric. Locate the center of fabric by folding in half top to bottom and again left to right. On the charted design, count the number of squares (stitches) from the center of the chart to where you wish to start. Then from the fabric's center, find your starting point by counting out the same number of fabric threads (stitches).

Recommended Colors: We refer to all colors by name and also by Anchor stranded cotton and DMC embroidery floss numbers. Cover model was stitched using DMC. Anchor numbers were chosen to assure proper blending of colors in the design and not as perfect matches to DMC. For this reason, we do not recommend that both brands be used in the same design.

STITCHING TIPS

Preparing Fabric: Being sure to allow plenty of margin, cut fabric desired size and overcast raw edges. It is better to waste a little fabric than to come up short after hours of stitching!

Preparing Thread: When working with embroidery thread, separate strands; then realign them before threading needle. This gives a smoother stitch. Keep stitching tension consistent. Begin and end thread by running under several stitches on back; never tie knots.

Number Of Strands: To determine the number of strands to use, see table below. These are merely suggestions; experiment to get the look you desire.

Thread Count Per Inch of Fabric	Number of Strands		
	Cross Stitch	Half Cross	Backstitch
Aida 11 or Hardanger 22 over 2	2 or 3	2	2 or 3
Aida 14 or Lugana 25 over 2	2 or 3	1	1 or 2
Aida 18	1 or 2	1	1 or 2
Hardanger 22	1	1	1

STITCH DIAGRAMS

Counted Cross Stitch: For horizontal rows, work Cross Stitches in two journeys **(Fig. 1)**. For vertical rows, complete each stitch as shown **(Fig. 2)**. When working over two fabric threads, work Cross Stitch as shown in **Fig. 3**. When the chart shows a Backstitch crossing a colored square **(Fig. 4)**, a Cross Stitch **(Fig. 1, 2 or 3)** should be worked first, then the Backstitch **(Fig. 7)** should be worked on top of the Cross Stitch.

Fig. 1

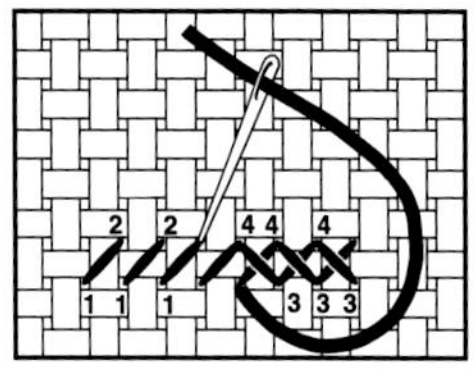

Fig. 2

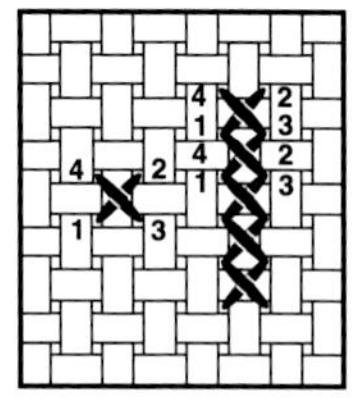

Fig. 3

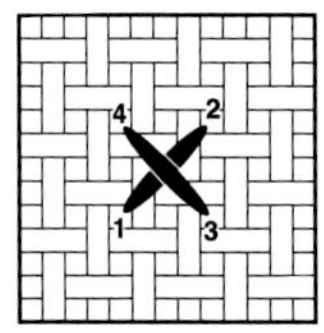

Fig.4

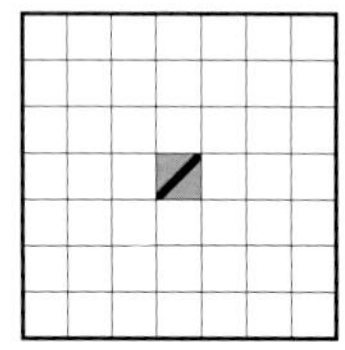

Half Cross Stitch: This stitch is one journey of the Cross Stitch and is worked from lower left to upper right as shown in **Fig. 5**. When working over two fabric threads, work Half Cross Stitch as shown in **Fig. 6**.

Fig. 5

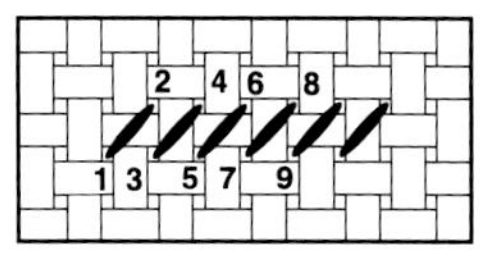

Fig. 6

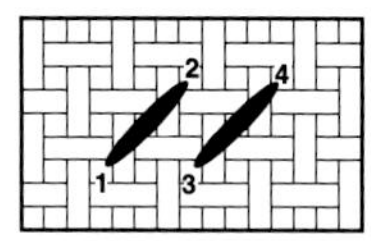

Backstitch: For outline detail, Backstitch (shown on chart and on color key by black or colored straight lines) should be worked after the design has been completed **(Fig. 7)**.

Fig. 7

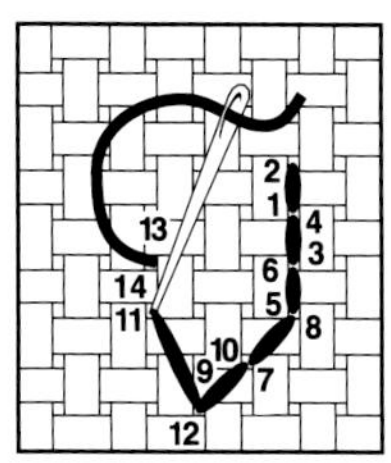

PROJECT

Footprints In The Sand - Mushroom Lugana - stitched over two fabric threads - approx design size 9 1/8" x 15 7/8" - custom framed.

We have made every effort to ensure that these instructions are accurate and complete. We cannot, however, be responsible for human error, typographical mistakes, or variations in individual work.

Made in U.S.A.